17 More Prehistoric Beasts

EVERYONE SHOULD KNOW ABOUT

STANTON F. FINK

VOLUME II OF STANTON'S COLORING BOOKS

Acknowledgments
and Dedication

To my father, in whose books I discovered my first monsters.

To Will Caligan, whose help and encouragement is one of the primary reasons for this coloring book's existence.

To Mariano Silvera, who should have had his own artbooks

To Doctor David Morafka, who helped teach me to be more picky with my information.

To my friends, who helped push me to make this.

Table of Contents

Introduction

The purpose of this coloring book series is to provide information on various prehistoric animals both profoundly famous and incredibly obscure to artists of all ages. Of course, there is a lot of material to work with, as animals have been a major component of Earth's ecosystems for at least 670 million years.

For the sake of space and workability, each volume will contain 17 entries: ideally, one species for each geological time period, if possible. If you, or your inner and or outer child do not see your favorite prehistoric animal here, it may be eventually featured in another volume. Or, contact me to have it put into a later volume.

Glossary

- **Aquatic**- Living in water.
- **Arthropod**- Any member of the animal phylum Arthropoda, including trilobites, arachnids, crustaceans, insects, myriapods and their relatives. All arthropods have armor-like, jointed exoskeletons made of chitin-derived plates, sometimes reinforced with calcium carbonate, and jointed limbs.
- **Biofilm**- A thin layer of scum made up of microscopic organisms, particularly fungi, bacteria and algae.
- **Brachiopod**- A superficially-clam-like marine animal that filterfeed. Even though brachiopods resemble mollusks, they are more closely related to bryozoans, or moss animals.
- **Browser**- In the context of herbivory, browsing is where the herbivore feeds on high-growing vegetation, i.e., eating leaves, shoots, twigs and bark from trees.
- **Cambrian**- A period of time in the Paleozoic Era from 541 to 485 million years ago.
- **Carapace**- A large shell or shell-like plate, or a series of plates or scales that form a shell-like structure over the dorsal side of an animal's thorax. Turtles, crabs, and heterostracan agnathans are examples of animals with carapaces.
- **Carboniferous**- A period of time in the Paleozoic Era from 359 to 300 million years ago.
- **Cenozoic**- An era of time in the Phanerozoic Eon from 65 million years ago until now.
- **Chordate**- Any member of the animal phylum Chordata, including sea squirts, lancet fish, and vertebrates (such as lampreys, sharks, tuna, frogs, lizards, chickens, and people). All chordates have, at least at some point in their life cycle, a notochord, a long, flexible rod, usually made of cartilage, or, in the case of most vertebrates, cartilage and bone, running down the back from head to tail, directly beneath the neural tube.
- **Cretaceous**- The last period of time in the Mesozoic Era, from 144 to 66 million years ago.
- **Devonian**- A period of time in the Paleozoic Era from 414 to 360 million years ago.
- **Ediacaran**- The last period of time in the Precambrian Eon from 635 to 542 million years ago.
- **Eocene**- A period of time in the Cenozoic Era from 55 to 33 million years ago.
- **Fauna**- In an ecological context, "fauna" refers to the animal components of an ecosystem.
- **Formation**- In a geological or paleontological context, a formation is a group of rock layers.
- **Gnathostome**- A gnathostome is any vertebrate chordate with a moveable jaw (or had an ancestor with one).
- **Holocene**- A period of time in the Cenozoic Era from 12,000 years ago until now.
- ***Incertae sedis***- A Latin phrase literally meaning "uncertain seat." *"Incertae sedis"* is a

term in classification used to refer to a species or group whose relationships with related organisms are unclear or poorly defined.

- **Jurassic**- The second period of time in the Mesozoic Era, from 199 to 145 million years ago.
- **Mesozoic**- An era of time in the Phanerozoic Eon from 249 to 66 million years ago.
- **Miocene**- A period of time in the Cenozoic Era from 23 to 5 million years ago.
- **Mollusk**- Any member of the animal phylum Mollusca, including snails, clams, squid, octopuses, tusk shells and chitons. Most mollusks have a calcium carbonate shell, and a toothed, file-like tongue called a radula. All mollusks have a cape-like organ, the mantle, which usually secretes the shell, and houses breathing organs, and a nervous system.
- **Nekton**- Any aquatic animal that lives either entirely or almost entirely in the water column, and relies on its own swimming or propulsion abilities to keep and move itself in and around the water column. Anchovies, porpoises and ichthyosaurs are examples of nekton.
- **Neogene**- The second third of the Cenozoic Era, comprising of the Miocene and the Pliocene periods.
- **Oligocene**- A period of time in the Cenozoic Era from 33 to 23 million years ago.
- **Ordovician**- A period of time in the Paleozoic Era from 484 to 440 million years ago.
- **Paleocene**- A period of time in the Cenozoic Era from 65 to 55 million years ago.
- **Paleogene**- The first third of the Cenozoic Era, comprising of the Paleocene, Eocene, and Oligocene.
- **Paleozoic**- An era of time in the Phanerozoic Eon from 249 to 66 million years ago.
- **Permian**- The last period of time in the Paleozoic Era, the time of "The Great Dying," or most severe of all known extinction events, from 299 to 250 million years ago.
- **Plankton**- An organism that uses water currents and waterflow to as its primary means of transportation in the water column because it is either too small to move long distances by its own power, or lacks the ability to propel itself entirely. Sargassum seaweed and jellyfish are two varieties of plankton.
- **Pleistocene**- A period of time in the Cenozoic Era from 3 million years ago until 12 thousand years ago.
- **Pliocene**- A period of time in the Cenozoic Era from 5 to 3 million years ago.
- **Quaternary**- The last third of the Cenozoic Era, comprising of the Pleistocene and the Holocene periods.
- **Terrestrial**- Living on land.
- **Triassic**- The first period of time in the Mesozoic Era, from 249 to 200 million years ago.

Name

Palmleaf Proarticulatan

Species	*Epibaion axifera*
Phylum	Proarticulata
Class	Dipleurozoa
Family	Dickinsoniidae
Size	Up to 44 cm by 34 cm
Time Period	Late Ediacaran of the Precambrian, 560 million years ago
Location	Arkhangelsk District, Zimnii Coast of the White Sea, Russia

Comments

The Palmleaf Proarticulatan, *Epibaion axifera*, is a mysterious member of a mysterious group of Late Precambrian organisms called "Proarticulata." The typical proarticulatan was a sac-like, fluid-filled creature built like a bilaterally symmetrical quilted air mattress, with one side being "off" by half of a segment, or isomere. Proarticulatans are thought to have moved around through microscopic cilia similar to those possessed by modern-day planarians and placozoans.

Despite having no mouths, proarticulatans are thought to have "eaten" food by releasing digestive enzymes out of their bottom-sides in order to digest the bacterial biofilms they rested and moved about upon, whereupon the digested material would be reabsorbed through osmosis, and stored inside of simple- to complex-shaped "guts" in the center of their bodies. These feeding traces are distinctive, and many sets can be identified to which species made them.

The feeding traces of the palmleaf proarticulatan (center) are very similar to those of *Dickinsonia* proarticulatans, such as of *D. tenuis*, at bottom, but differ in the shape and orientation of the isomeres. Feeding traces of *Yorgia* (top) can be easily identified by their circular shape.

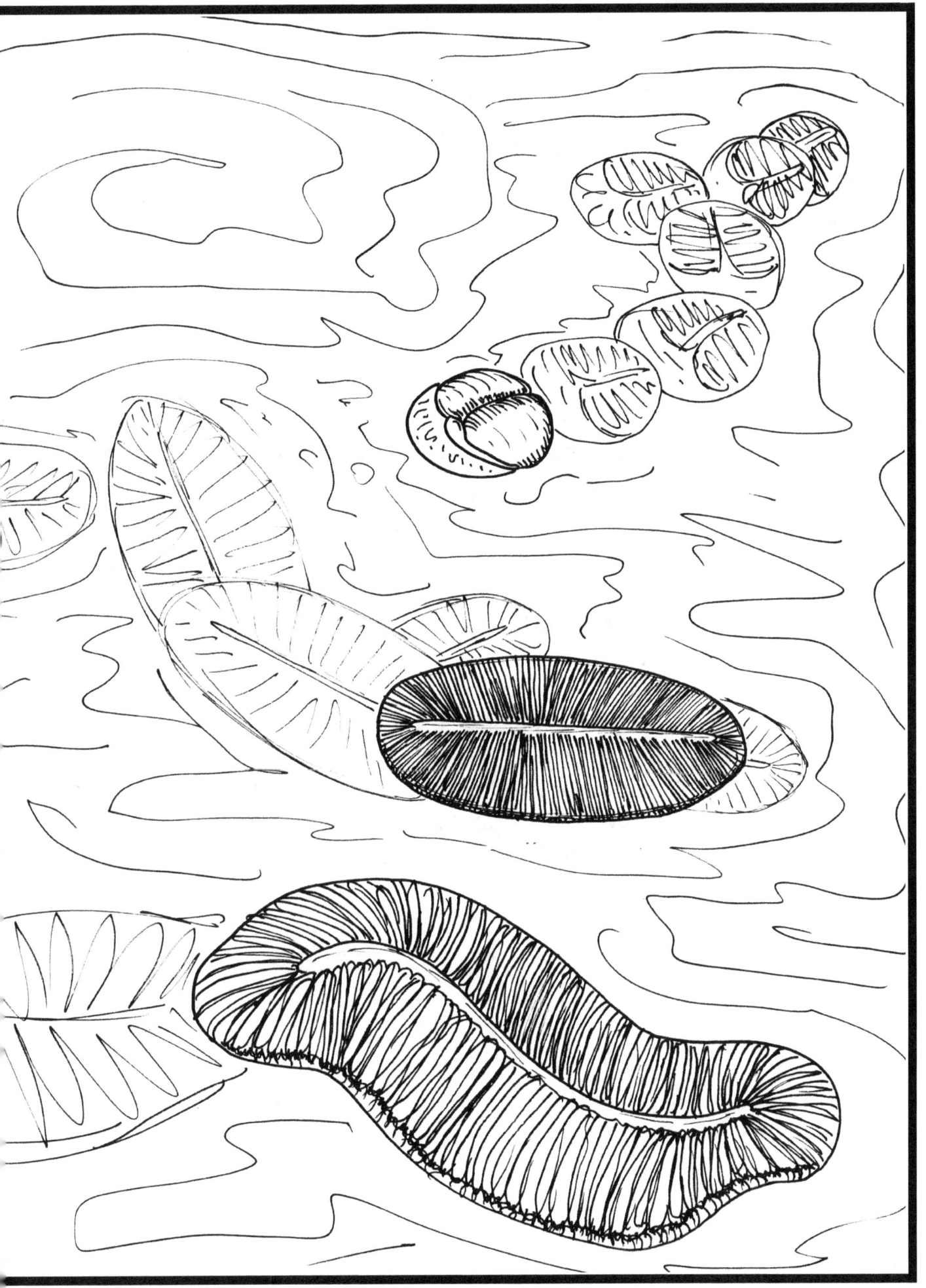

Name
Measured Meteor Trilobite

Species   *Meteoraspis metra*

Phylum   Arthropoda

Class   Trilobita

Order   Ptychopariidae

Family   Tricrepicephalidae

Size   Up to 3 centimeters long

Time Period Dresbachian epoch of the Late Cambrian, 501 to 490 million years ago

Location   Texas, and South Dakota of the United States of America

Comments   The fossils of the various species of meteor trilobites are found in numerous Dresbachian-aged marine strata throughout the United States, China, Japan, Australia and Antarctica, demonstrating that the meteor trilobites had a significant role in several marine ecologies during the Late Cambrian.

Meteor trilobites lived in deepwater environments composed of diverse communities of other trilobites and brachiopods. Meteor trilobites, themselves, probably ate detritus or small organisms. The Measured meteor trilobite is found in Dresbachian-aged shales in the states of Texas and South Dakota.

Name	Gog's Trilobite
Species	*Gog catillus*
Phylum	Arthropoda
Class	Trilobita
Order	Asaphida
Family	Asaphidae
Size	Up to 10 centimeters
Time Period	Late Arenig epoch of the Ordovician, around 471 million years ago
Location	Valhallfonna Formation of Spitbergen, Norway
Comments	The Gog's Trilobite is named after a Biblical figure of obscure description who inspired the legend of the British giant, Gogmagog.

The Gog's Trilobite is named after a Biblical figure of obscure description who inspired the legend of the British giant, Gogmagog.

Gog's trilobite is closely related to asaphid trilobites of the genus *Niobe*, and anatomical features suggest the Gog's is a transitional form between *Niobe* asaphid trilobites and asaphid trilobites in the genus *Ogygiocaris*.

The large size of the Gog's trilobite suggests it probably ate smaller animals, including the many, many other trilobites found in Ordovician Spitsbergen at the time.

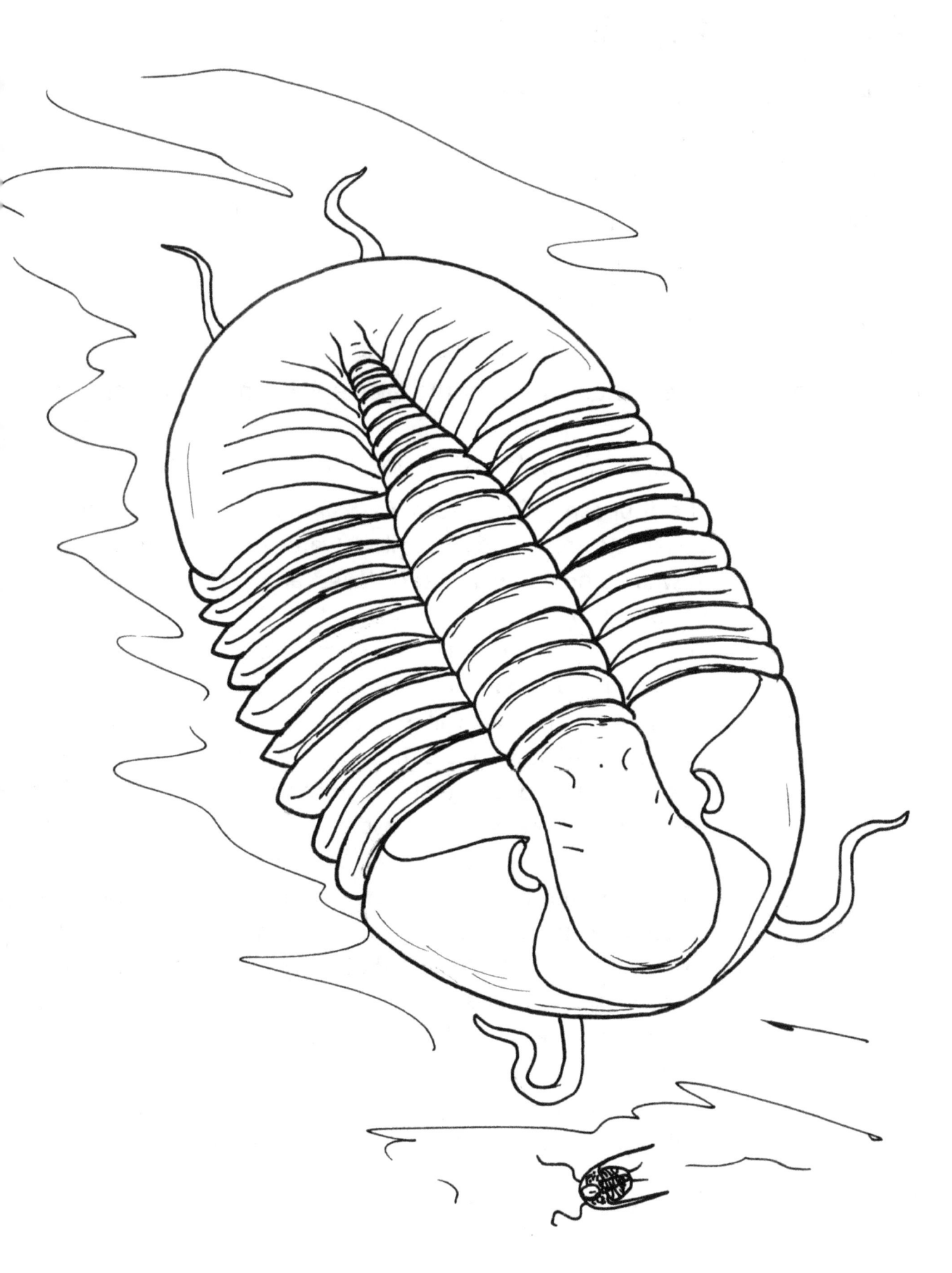

Name	Cupfish
Species	*Cyathaspis banksii*
Phylum	Chordata
Class	Pteraspidomorphi
Subclass	Heterostraci
Order	Cyathaspidiformes
Family	Cyathaspidae
Size	Up to 2 to 3 centimeters in length
Time Period	Late Ludlow epoch of the Middle Silurian, 423 million years ago
Location	Great Britain and possibly Gotland, Sweden
Comments	The Cupfish, *Cyathaspis banksii*, is a primitive jawless vertebrate that lived in shallow-water marine environments in what is now England and Wales, and possibly in Gotland, Sweden, too.

The cupfish embodies the typical heterostracan, or "armored agnathan" bodyplan. To a human, a live cupfish would have resembled very much like a tadpole, but with thick, bony scales. These scales were made of the tissues dentine, which is also found in the teeth of most vertebrates, including those of humans, and aspidine, a tissue unique to heterostracans. Unlike a frog tadpole, the cupfish did not have a sucker-like mouth. Its mouth, like those of other heterostracans, was a slot-like opening at the base of the rostrum, or nose-like plate, that allowed for the passage of certain-sized particles due to currents generated by the flow of water over a fringed lower lip composed of several small plates.

The cupfish used its specially adapted mouth to suck up edible particles from the sediment in its home environment on the seafloor.

Name	Scrimshark
Species	*Incisoscutum ritchiei*
Phylum	Chordata
Class	Placodermi
Order	Arthrodira
Family	Incisoscutidae
Size	About 30 to 40 centimeters in length
Time Period	Late Frasnian epoch of the Late Devonian period, 380 million years ago
Location	Gogo Reef, Western Australia
Comments	The Scrimshark, *Incisoscutum ritchiei*, is one of several placoderms endemic to the Gogo Reef Formation in what is now Western Australia. During the late Frasnian epoch, that region of Australia was underwater, and home to several barrier reefs composed of coral and stone-forming algae.

The scrimshark is one of the more common placoderms found in Gogo Reef, and their fossils are routinely exquisitely preserved. Several specimens have remains of other placoderms preserved in their abdominal regions. At first, this was taken as evidence that the scrimshark was a predator of other placoderms, and confirming that the sharp and powerful, beak-like jaws were for breaking their prey's armor. Closer, more detailed examinations showed that these remains did not show any damage suggestive of predation or digestion, suggesting, instead, that these were developing embryos, and that the placoderms they were inside of were their mothers. These fossil embryos, coupled with fossil embryos found in other, more distantly related placoderms, as well as delicate anatomy preserved in pristine fossils, show that placoderms performed internal fertilization and livebirth.

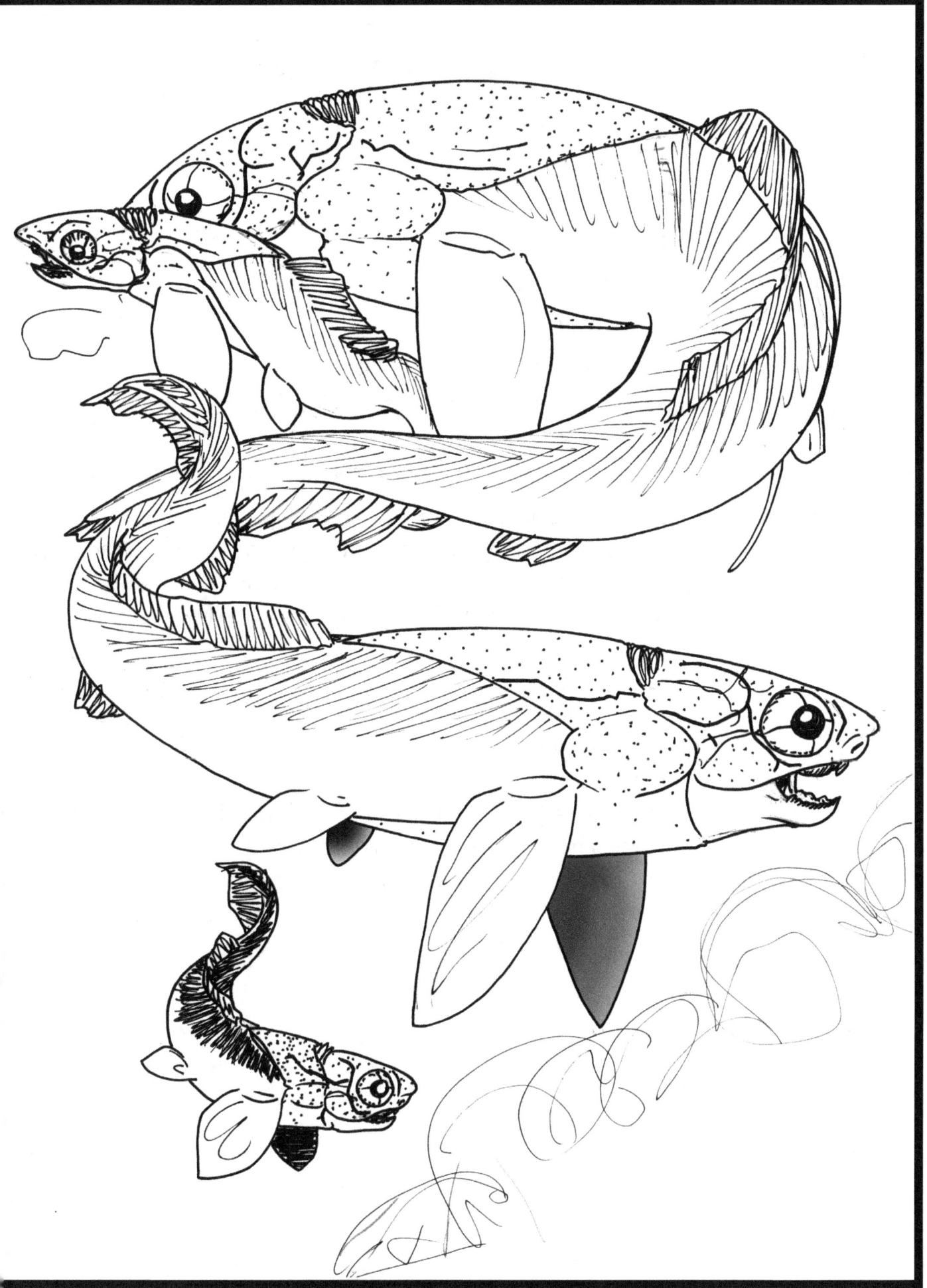

Name	Fringed Giant Millipede
Species	*Arthropleura cristata*
Phylum	Arthropoda
Subphylum	Myriapoda
Class	? Diplopoda
Order	Arthropleurida
Family	Arthropleuridae
Size	Estimated to be up to 1 meter in length
Time Period	Middle Pennsylvanian epoch of the Carboniferous, about 300 million years ago
Location	Braidwood Fauna of Mazon Creek, Grundy County, Illinois
Comments	The Arthropleurids, or "Giant Millipedes," are an extinct group of myriapods that either are primitive millipedes, or are closely related to millipedes. Giant millipedes of the genus *Arthropleura* were huge, forest-dwellers who are thought to have eaten lycopod clubmosses and primitive ferns. Coprolites, or fossilized feces found in the same strata as the exoskeleton fragments strongly suggest the living animals preferentially ate the spore-bearing portions of those plants. The Fringed giant millipede, *A. cristata*, is a medium-sized species from America, and is estimated to be about 1 meter in length (the Armored giant millipede, *A. armatus*, from Scotland, is estimated to be at least 2 meters long).

Name	Aras River Ammonite
Species	*Araxoceras latissimum*
Phylum	Mollusca
Class	Cephalopoda
Order	Ceratitida
Family	Araxoceratidae
Size	Shell is about 6 centimeters wide
Time Period	From the late Dzhulfian or Wuchiapingian epoch of the Permian, about 254 million years ago.
Location	Along the Aras River, in Northern Iran and Azerbaijan.
Comments	The Aras River Ammonite, *Araxoceras latissimum*, is one of numerous fossil species that are used as stratigraphical markers. A stratigraphical marker is a fossil that, because of its limited chronological range, is used by geologists and palaeontologists to identify a specific range of sedimentary layers. In the case of the Aras River Ammonite, its fossils are used to identify Latest Permian-aged marine strata in Northern Iran and Azerbaijan along the beds of the Aras River, and related species in other parts of Iran, the Caucasus Mountains of Armenia and Georgia, China and Japan are used to identify similarly-aged marine strata in those locations.

The Aras River Ammonite and its relatives form a lineage of ammonites that lived in shallow marine environments along the southern area of the Paleo-Tethys Ocean, an ancient ocean that existed along the northern coastline of Gondwana during the Paleozoic (and closed up at the end of the Triassic). The lineage of *Araxoceras* would go extinct soon after the Permian-Triassic extinction event.

The Aras River Ammonite is easily distinguished by its massive, flat keel, and voluminous, shelf-like margins.

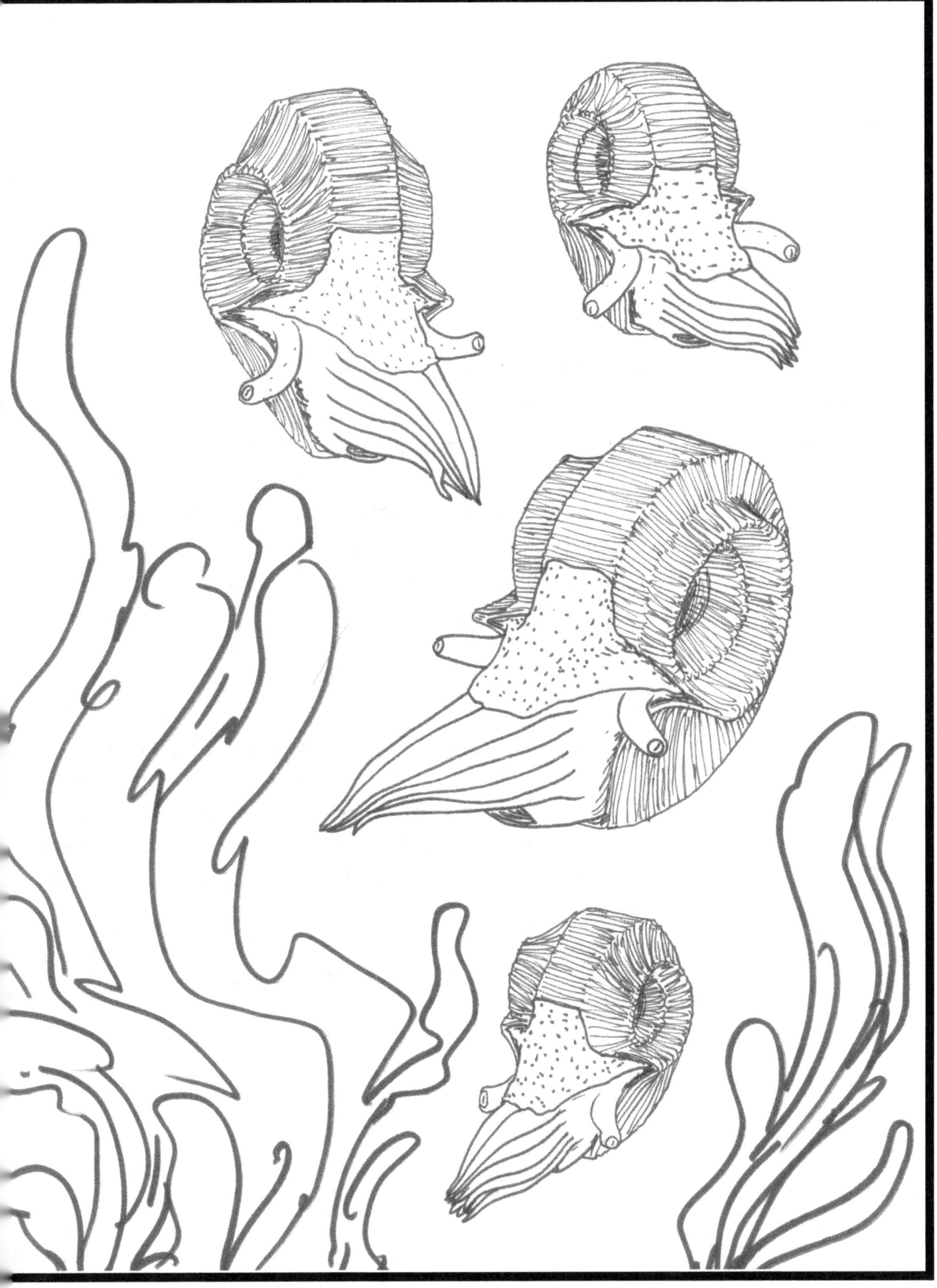

Name	Plaquiguana
Species	*Placodus gigas*
Phylum	Chordata
Class	Reptilia
Order	Placodontia
Family	Placodontidae
Size	Over 2 meters in length
Time Period	Middle Triassic, about 240 million years ago
Location	Central Europe
Comments	

The Plaquiguana, *Placodus gigas*, is one of the best known of the Placodonts, a clan of superficially lizard-like or turtle-like marine reptiles related to the Plesiosaurs, the Nothosaurs, and the Ichthyosaurs.

Most placodonts, including the plaquiguana, were adapted for swimming along the seafloor and feeding on shellfish. The plaquiguana had thick, heavy bones that made it negatively buoyant, allowing them to sink to the bottom very quickly whenever it stopped swimming with its paddle-like legs and long, sinuous tail. To help it prey on shellfish, the plaquiguana had peg-like incisors that would have allowed it great ease in plucking off bivalve mollusks or brachiopods that cemented themselves to a hard surface, and enormous, block-like back teeth that formed a large, pavement-like surface to crush shells with.

Another species, the Unexpected Plaquiguana, is known from similarly-aged marine strata in China.

Name	Prickly Kazakharthran
Species	*Iliella spinosa*
Phylum	Arthropoda
Subphylum	Crustacea
Class	Branchiopoda
Order	Kazacharthra
Family	Ketmeniidae
Size	Around 3 to 4 centimeters long
Time Period	Early Jurassic
Location	Ketmen Mountains of Kazakhstan

Comments

The Prickly Kazakharthran, *Iliella spinosa*, is one of several species of extinct, branchiopod crustaceans called "kazacharthrans," that lived in marshes, lakes and temporary ponds on an island off the coast of Pangaea that would eventually become what are today Kazakhstan and Xinjiang. When this island broke off from Pangaea during the late Triassic, notostracan tadpole shrimp present there evolved into kazakharthrans. Kazakharthrans are very similar to the ancestral tadpole shrimps, but differ in having paint pallet-shaped, guitar pick-shaped or fingernail-shaped, uniquely ornamented carapaces, and vestigial eyes that, in the adult, were nonfunctional beyond serving as an anchoring point for carapace muscles.

Despite these differences (and being blind as adults), kazakharthrans are thought to have lived lifestyles very similar to those of modern-day tadpole shrimp in that they were omnivores that opportunistically gobbled whatever edible material they found, including each other as this particular prickly kazakharthran demonstrates in the picture eating another prickly. The larger animal is the Great Thorny kazakharthran, *Panacanthocaris ketmenia*, and the smaller is the Jean Roger's kazakharthran, *Jeanrogerium sornayi*.

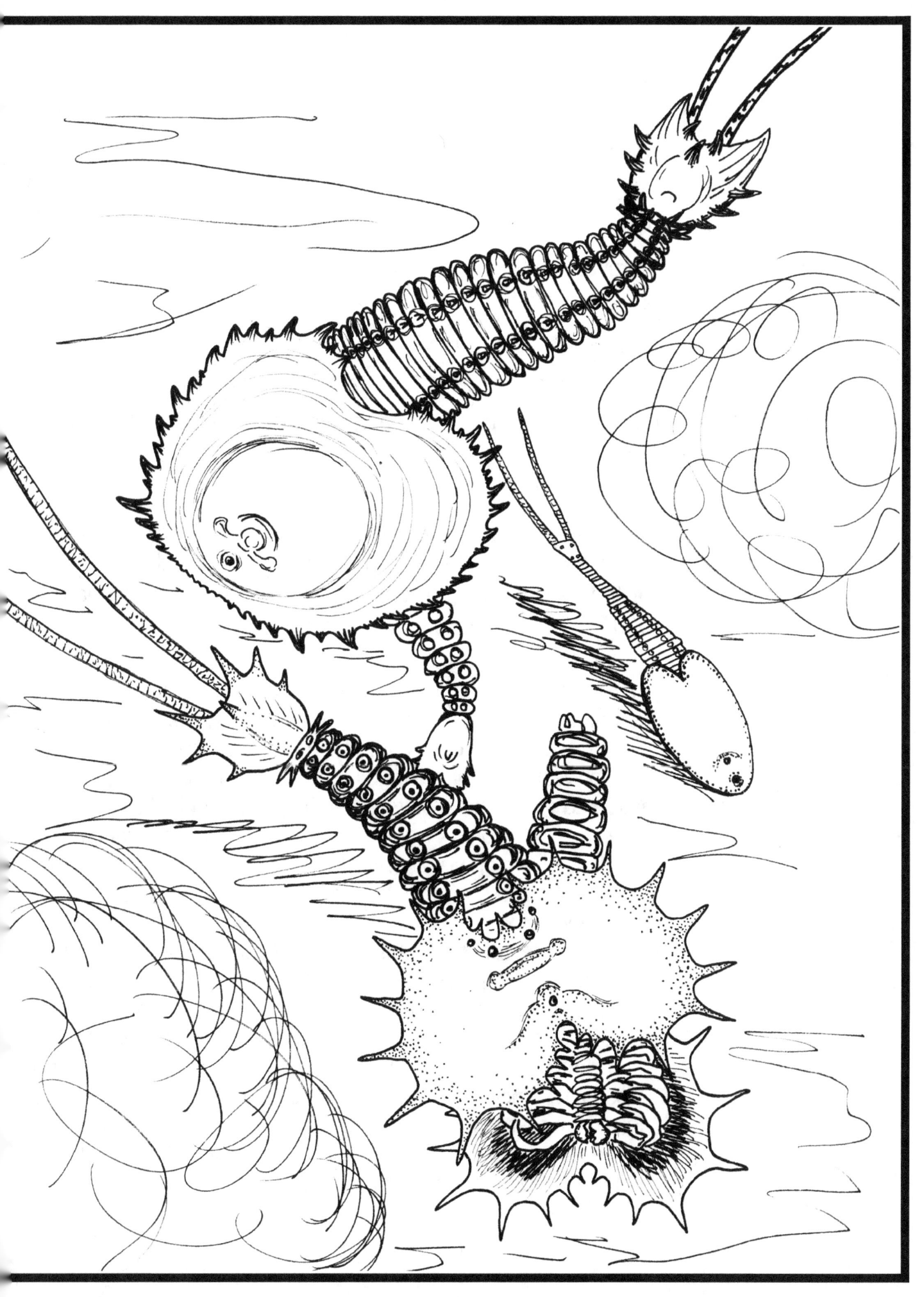

Name	Balaur
Species	*Balaur bondoc*
Phylum	Chordata
Class	Reptilia
"Clade"	Paraves
"Clade"	Avialae
"Clade"	Euavialae
Size	Estimated to be about 2 meters from snout to tail-tip
Time Period	Maastrichtian epoch of the Late Cretaceous, 70 million years ago
Location	"Haţeq Island" in what is now Romania

Comments

The Romanian Stocky Dragon, or "Balaur," *Balaur bondoc*, represents one of several "magic middles" of the spectrum of "this is clearly a (theropod) dinosaur" and "this is clearly a bird." When its fossil was first discovered, the balaur was originally described as an island-dwelling dromeosaur theropod dinosaur that lived on an island where Haţeq, Romania is today. Odd anatomy, such as having two retractable sickle claws on the hindfoot, rather than one, and a vestigial third finger on an atrophied hand, were assumed to be the results of evolution on an isolated island. Later, its anatomy was reexamined, and the balaur is reassessed as being a primitive bird, or "avian (theropod) dinosaur" more bird-like than the dromeosaurs or *Archaeopteryx*.

The lifestyle of the balaur has been subject to much research and educated speculation, as its overall similarity to the dromeosaurs, particularly its massive sickle clawed toes, suggest it was a predator, while its close relationship to primitive, non-carnivorous birds like *Sapeornis* and *Jeholornis*, together with the articulations of its hand and pelvis suggest it was not carnivorous. Its large size strongly suggests it was flightless, though, its immediate ancestor is hypothesized to have flown to Haţeq Island.

# Name	# Horned Alligator
Species	*Ceratosuchus burdoshi*
Phylum	Chordata
Class	Reptilia
Order	Crocodilia
Family	Alligatoridae
Size	Possibly up to 2 meters long
Time Period	Clarkfordian Epoch, latest Paleocene to Earliest Eocene, 56 million years ago
Location	Latest Paleocene from Piceance Basin, Colorado, and Earliest Eocene from Bighorn Basin, Wyoming
Comments	The Horned Alligator, *Ceratosuchus burdoshi*, of Paleogene United States of America, is one of a handful of crocodilian species that had wing-like "horns" that developed from modified scutes on the back of the head. The shape and angle of the horns, as well as the lack of sharp points obviously show that they were not used as weapons, and that their small size suggests that they were not used to intimidate. Researchers, instead, suspect that the horns of the horned alligator were used to recognize other individuals of the same species, as the horned alligator coexisted with alligators of the extinct genus *Allognathosuchus* (like *A. wartheni* in the picture).

The horned alligator, like other small-sized crocodilians, probably ate a wide variety of fish and freshwater invertebrates.

Name	French Cerberus
Species	*Kerberos langebadreae*
Phylum	Chordata
Class	Mammalia
Order	Hyaenodontida
Family	Hyainailuridae
Size	Skull about 30 centimeters long, estimated to be 140 kilograms in weight
Time Period	Middle Eocene, 41 to 38 million years ago
Location	Near Montespieu, in Tarn, France
Comments	The French Cerberus, *Kerberus langebadreae*, is a large hyaenodont of the family Hyainailuridae from the Middle Eocene of France. Hyaenodonts are an extinct group of predatory mammals that apparently originated in Africa during the Paleocene, then spread to Eurasia and North America, and persisted there, competing and eventually ecologically displacing the mesonychids, until the hyaenodonts were, themselves, displaced ecologically by predatory carnivoran mammals during the Miocene.

The skull and teeth of the French cerberus are those of a meat-eating, bone-crunching predator. Postcranial remains suggested it stalked and ran down prey like a lion or a wolf. Researchers hypothesize that the French cerberus may have preyed on other, smaller, weasel-like and fox-like hyaenodonts.

Name	Glarus Jack
Species	*Archaeus glarisianus*
Phylum	Chordata
Class	Actinopterygii
Order	Perciformes
Family	Carangidae
Size	3 to 10 centimeters long
Time Period	Early to Middle Rupellian epoch of the Early Oligocene, 33 to 30 million years ago
Location	Central Europe, especially Switzerland
Comments	The Glarus Jack, *Archaeus glarisianus*, is an extinct jackfish from the Early Oligocene that lived in the northwestern reaches of the Tethys Ocean in what is now Central Europe. A related species from the Late Paleocene, the Oblong Jack, *A. oblongus*, lived in the central region of the Tethys in what is now Turkmenistan.

The Glarus Jack, named after Canton Glarus, where the best specimens have been collected, lived, and apparently died in large schools. Numerous different species of *Archaeus* jackfish have been described from fossils, but, almost all of them have been reappraised as different specimens of the Glarus Jack in different degrees of decay and deformation.

Name	Brahma's Giraffe
Species	*Bramatherium perimense*
Phylum	Chordata
Class	Mammalia
Order	Artiodactyla
Family	Giraffidae
Size	Similar in size to a large domesticated bull
Time Period	Late Miocene to Pliocene, about 7 to 3 million years ago
Location	Southern and Western Asia, from India to Turkey

Comments

Brahma's Giraffe, *Bramatherium perimense*, is a close relative of the Siva's Giraffes of the genus *Sivatherium*. In life, the Brahma's giraffe would have resembled a cattle-sized okapi with a crown-like set of ossicones.

As with living giraffes and okapis, the Brahma's giraffe was was a tree-nibbling, browsing herbivore that reached for especially tasty leaves and twigs with a long, prehensile tongue and fleshy, prehensile lips.

The Brahma's giraffe was named in honor of the Hindu god Brahma just as the Siva's giraffe was named for Siva, as the first specimens of both animals were found in India. There is a Vishnu's giraffe, *Vishnutherium iravadicum*, but, very little is known about it beyond a left half of a lower jaw found from Late Miocene Burma.

Name	Hyraxipotamus
Species	*Kvabebihyrax kachethicus*
Phylum	Chordata
Class	Mammalia
Order	Hyracoidea
Family	Pliohyracidae
Size	About one and a half meters long, similar in size to a large domesticated pig
Time Period	Late Pliocene, about 3 million years ago
Location	Kvabebi, Georgia, in the Caucasus Mountains
Comments	Hyrax fossils show that there was once an enormous diversity among hyraxes in both size and ecological roles. The Hyraxipotamus, *Kvabebihyrax kachethicus*, easily demonstrates this now-lost diversity. The hyraxipotamus was a large animal about as big as a domesticated pig and was, unusually for a hyrax, adapted for a semi-aquatic lifestyle feeding on freshwater plants. These adaptations include eyes, nose and ears set high on the head, and a robustly built body similar to that of a hippopotamus.

Name Rusinga Island Wildebeest

Species   *Rusingoryx atopocranion*

Phylum   Chordata

Class   Mammalia

Order   Artiodactyla

Family   Bovidae

Size   Probably 120 to 150 centimeters at the shoulders

Time Period Late Pleistocene, about 41 to 28 thousand years ago

Location   Wakondo, Rusinga Island, Kenya

Comments   The Rusinga Island Wildebeest, sometimes called the "Dinosaur Wildebeest," *Rusingoryx atopocranion*, is a peculiar antelope closely related to the living wildebeests of the genus *Connochaetes*. Because of its peculiar head, the Rusinga Island wildebeest was once classified into the giant wildebeest genus *Megalotragus*. Further study of the skull noted that the nasal passages were comparatively huge, leading researchers to keep the Rusinga Island wildebeest in its own distinct genus. The enlarged nasal passages would have allowed the living animal to make very loud, far-ranging, and resonating calls in a similar manner to the way crested hadrosaur dinosaurs are hypothesized to have made with their hollow crests.

Damaged bones found with stone tools demonstrate that the animals were hunted and butchered by Middle Stone Age humans.

Name	# Giant Tapir
Species	*Megatapirus augustus*
Phylum	Chordata
Class	Mammalia
Order	Perissodactyla
Family	Tapiridae
Size	90 centimeters at the shoulder, 210 centimeters long, similar in size to an Indian rhinoceros
Time Period	Early Pleistocene to 2000 BCE, from about 1.5 million to 4000 years ago
Location	Southern China and Vietnam
Comments	The Giant Tapir, *Megatapirus augustus*, is an extinct, rhinoceros-sized tapir that lived in tropical forests of Southern China and Vietnam. Despite the fact that it went extinct during historical times, humans did not know of it until the first fossils were discovered in 1923: written references to tapir-like animals in ancient Chinese and Vietnamese texts all appear to refer to the still-living Malaysian tapir, *Tapirus indicus*, (depicted below the giant tapir in the picture).

Tapirs were more diverse during the Pleistocene than they are today, as several, now extinct tapir species were found throughout North America, as well as Southern Asia and South America. The giant tapir was not directly related to the Malaysian tapir, and was, according to examination of various fossil skulls, instead descended from a line of Chinese tapir species that lived during the Late Pliocene and Early Pleistocene.

Bibliography

- Bannikov, A. F., and N. N. Parin. "The list of marine fishes from Cenozoic (Upper Paleocene-Middle Miocene) localities in southern European Russia and adjacent countries." *Journal of Ichthyology* 37.2 (1997): 133-146.

- Bartels, William S. (1984). "Osteology and systematic affinities of the horned alligator *Ceratosuchus* (Reptilia, Crocodylia)". *Journal of Paleontology*. **58** (6): 1347–1353.

- Bate, R. H., et al. "Arthropoda: Crustacea." *Geological Society, London, Special Publications* 2.1 (1967): 535-563.

- Cau, Andrea, Tom Brougham, and Darren Naish. "The phylogenetic affinities of the bizarre Late Cretaceous Romanian theropod Balaur bondoc (Dinosauria, Maniraptora): dromaeosaurid or flightless bird?." *PeerJ* 3 (2015): e1032.

- Csiki, Zoltán, et al. "An aberrant island-dwelling theropod dinosaur from the Late Cretaceous of Romania." *Proceedings of the National Academy of Sciences* 107.35 (2010): 15357-15361.

- Faith, J. Tyler, et al. "Taxonomic status and paleoecology of Rusingoryx atopocranion (Mammalia, Artiodactyla), an extinct Pleistocene bovid from Rusinga Island, Kenya." Quaternary Research 75.3 (2011): 697-707

- Fortey, R., and Skrifter, N. "The Ordovician Trilobites of Spitsbergen."

- Geraads, Denis, and Erksin Güleç. "A Bramatherium skull (Giraffidae, Mammalia) from the late Miocene of Kavakdere (Central Turkey). Biogeographic and phylogenetic implications." *Mineral Res. Expl. Bul* 121 (1999): 51-56.

- Haley D. O'Brien, J. Tyler Faith, Kirsten E. Jenkins, Daniel J. Peppe, Thomas W. Plummer, Zenobia L. Jacobs, Bo Li, Renaud Joannes-Boyau, Gilbert Price, Yue-xing Feng and Christian A. Tryon (2016). "Unexpected Convergent Evolution of Nasal Domes between Pleistocene Bovids and Cretaceous Hadrosaur Dinosaurs". *Current Biology*. **26** (4): 503–508

- Haowen, Tong, Liu Jinyi, and Han Ligang. "On fossil remains of early Pleistocene tapir (Perissodactyla, Mammalia) from Fanchang, Anhui." Chinese Science Bulletin 47.7 (2002): 586-590.

- Ivantsov, A. Yu. (April 2007). "Small Vendian transversely Articulated fossils". *Paleontological Journal*. **41** (2): 113

- Khan, Muhammad Akbar, Muhammad Akhtar, and Ammara Irum. "Bramatherium (Artiodactyla, Ruminantia, Giraffidae) from the Middle Siwaliks of Hasnot, Pakistan: biostratigraphy and palaeoecology." *Turkish Journal of Earth Sciences* 23.3 (2014): 308-320.

- Long, John A., Kate Trinajstic, and Zerina Johanson. "Devonian arthrodire embryos and the origin of internal fertilization in vertebrates." *Nature* 457.7233 (2009): 1124-1127.

- Novitskaya, L. I. "Evolution of generic and species diversity in agnathans (Heterostraci: Orders Cyathaspidiformes, Pteraspidiformes)." *Paleontological Journal* 41.3 (2007): 268-

280.

- Rieppel, O. (2002). Feeding mechanisms in Triassic stem-group sauropterygians: the anatomy of a successful invasion of Mesozoic seas Zoological Journal of the Linnean Society, 135, 33-63

- Solé, Floréal, et al. "A new large hyainailourine from the Bartonian of Europe and its bearings on the evolution and ecology of massive hyaenodonts (Mammalia)." *PloS one* 10.9 (2015): e0135698.

- Stitt, J.H.; Perfetta, P.J. (2000). "Trilobites, Biostratigraphy, and Lithostratigraphy of the Crepicephalus and Aphelaspis zones, Lower Deadwood formation (Marjuman and Steptoean Stages, Upper Cambrian), Black Hills, South Dakota". *Journal of Paleontology.* **74** (2): 199–223

- Schwartz, Gary T., D. Tab Rasmussen, and Richard J. Smith. "Body-size diversity and community structure of fossil hyracoids." *Journal of Mammalogy* 76.4 (1995): 1088-1099.

- Wittry, Jack. The Mazon Creek Fossil Fauna. Esconi, 2012.

- Zakharov, Yuri D., Alexander M. Popov, and Alexander S. Biakov. "Late Permian to Middle Triassic palaeogeographic differentiation of key ammonoid groups: evidence from the former USSR." *Polar Research* 27.3 (2008): 441-468.

About the Artist

Stanton F. Fink is a student of Biology and Chinese Medicine, and makes a hobby of drawing monsters and researching flowers, arcane-looking creatures, prehistoric animals, fish, reptiles, birds and the occasional, really grotesque fungal fruiting body.

Stanton grew up and went to school in California and is currently living, drawing, and gardening in Oregon.

www.ingramcontent.com/pod-product-compliance
Lightning Source LLC
Chambersburg PA
CBHW081758280526
45789CB00008B/2901